CROCHET BABY

Publications International, Ltd.

Consulting by Heidi Beazley

Written by Beth Taylor

Photo styling by Amy Stark and Kelsey Faletto

Photography by Christopher Hiltz, except pages 4, 8 from Shutterstock.com

Crochet symbols and abbreviations from Craft Yarn Council's www.YarnStandards.com

Louis Weber, CEO
Publications International, Ltd.
8140 Lehigh Avenue
Morton Grove, IL 60053

Permission is never granted for commercial purposes.

ISBN: 978-1-68022-807-6

Manufactured in China.

8 7 6 5 4 3 2 1

TABLE OF CONTENTS

SUPPLIES
HOOKS, YARN & MATERIALS

What You'll Need

Crochet Hooks

Crochet hooks can be made from aluminum, plastic, wood, or bamboo. They are available in a wide range of sizes and are used with an assortment of yarns. Steel hooks are the smallest and are often used with fine thread in delicate crochet work, such as lace and doilies. Most patterns and yarn labels recommend a hook size. Select a crochet hook that feels comfortable to you and works well with your project and yarn.

Common Hook Sizes

U.S.	B-1	C-2	D-3	E-4	F-5	G-6	7	H-8	I-9	J-10	K-10.5	L-11	M-13	N-15	P	Q	S
mm	2.25	2.75	3.25	3.5	3.75	4	4.5	5	5.5	6	6.5	8	9	10	15	16	19

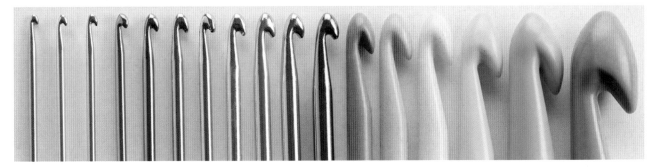

Needles

Tapestry or yarn needles have a blunt tip and an eye large enough to accommodate thick yarns. These special needles can be used to weave in yarn ends or sew crocheted pieces together.

Stitch Markers

As their name suggests, stitch markers are designed to mark your stitches. They can be used to mark a certain number of stitches, the beginning of a round, or where to make a particular stitch. Stitch markers must have openings so that they can be easily removed. You can purchase stitch markers, or improvise with pins, earrings, or safety pins.

Pins

Use long, rustproof pins for blocking and pinning seams together. Pins can also serve as stitch markers. Opt for pins with large, colorful heads that won't get lost in your crochet work.

Measurement Tools

Measuring tape is a must-have tool when taking body measurements before making garments. Measuring tape and rulers can be used to measure gauge.

All About Yarn

Yarn for Beginners

Before starting any new crochet project, you must select your yarn. For beginners learning the basic stitches, select a simple cotton yarn that is light colored, smooth, and sturdy. It's harder to see your stitches with dark colored yarn. Avoid fuzzy and loosely woven yarns that fray easily.

Yarn Fibers

Natural fibers

Cotton, linen, and hemp yarns are made from plant fibers. They are lightweight, breathable, and machine washable. Mercerized cotton has undergone a chemical process that results in stronger, shinier yarn.

Yarns made from animal fibers include wool, silk, cashmere, mohair, alpaca, and angora. These animal fibers are much warmer than plant fibers. Both types of natural fibers offer a bit of stretch.

Synthetic fibers

Yarns made from synthetic fibers include nylon, rayon, acrylic, and polyester. Synthetic yarns are usually less expensive than natural fibers, but are less breathable and pill more easily.

Novelty and specialty yarns

Novelty and specialty yarns can be tricky to work with, but create a distinctive look. They include bouclé, ladder, eyelash, and chenille. While great for trims and accessories, novelty yarn is not best for beginners.

Selecting Your Yarn

Each package of store-bought yarn has a label listing the yarn's length, fiber content, and weight. Yarn weight refers to the thickness of a yarn. It ranges from the thinnest embroidery thread to the bulkiest yarn. Yarn labels also recommend hook size—just look for the crochet hook symbol to find the U.S. and metric hook size.

Yarn Weight Guidelines

Yarn types: Fingering, lace, and 10-count crochet thread
Recommended hook sizes (metric): 1.5–2.25 mm
Recommended hook sizes (U.S.): Steel 6 to B-1
Crochet gauge range: 32–42 double crochet stitches to 4 in.

Yarn types: Sock, fingering, and baby
Recommended hook sizes (metric): 2.25–3.5 mm
Recommended hook sizes (U.S.): B-1 to E-4
Crochet gauge range: 21–32 single crochet stitches to 4 in.

Yarn types: Sport and baby
Recommended hook sizes (metric): 3.5–4.5 mm
Recommended hook sizes (U.S.): E-4 to 7
Crochet gauge range: 16–20 single crochet stitches to 4 in.

Yarn types: Double knitting and light worsted
Recommended hook sizes (metric): 4.5–5.5 mm
Recommended hook sizes (U.S.): 7 to I-9
Crochet gauge range: 12–17 single crochet stitches to 4 in.

Yarn types: Afghan, aran, and worsted
Recommended hook sizes (metric): 5.5–6.5 mm
Recommended hook sizes (U.S.): I-9 to K-10.5
Crochet gauge range: 11–14 single crochet stitches to 4 in.

Yarn types: Chunky, craft, and rug
Recommended hook sizes (metric): 6.5–9 mm
Recommended hook sizes (U.S.): K-10.5 to M-13
Crochet gauge range: 8–11 single crochet stitches to 4 in.

Yarn types: Bulky and roving
Recommended hook sizes (metric): 9–15 mm
Recommended hook sizes (U.S.): M-13 to Q
Crochet gauge range: 7–9 single crochet stitches to 4 in.

Yarn types: Jumbo and roving
Recommended hook sizes (metric): 15 mm and larger
Recommended hook sizes (U.S.): Q and larger
Crochet gauge range: 6 single crochet stitches and fewer to 4 in.

Source: Craft Yarn Council's www.YarnStandards.com

THE BASICS
GETTING STARTED

Holding the Hook

Pencil Hold

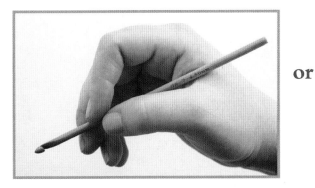

or

Knife Hold

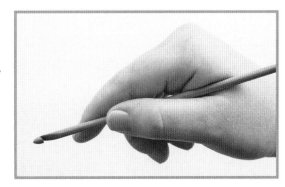

Tip: The instructions and photographs in this book are intended for right-handed crocheters. If you are a lefty, try holding up a mirror to the edge of a photograph to see the left-handed version.

Holding the Yarn

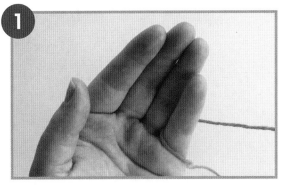

With your palm facing up, weave the working yarn (the yarn coming from the ball) between your pinky and ring fingers. Wrap the yarn clockwise around your pinky.

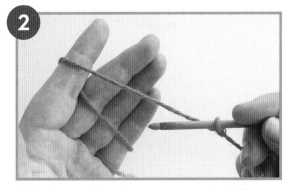

Take the yarn across your ring and middle fingers. Then wrap the yarn under and around your index finger.

Hold the yarn under the slip knot with your left thumb and middle finger.

Tip: There are many ways to hold your yarn. Experiment with different methods until you find what is most comfortable for you.

Making a Slip Knot

The first step in any crochet project is a slip knot.
The slip knot is what attaches the yarn to your hook.

Wrap the yarn around your index and middle fingers on your yarn hand to create an X.

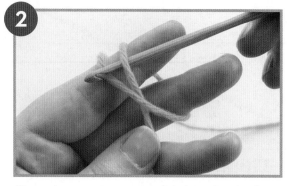

From the top, insert your hook under the first loop to grab the second loop.

Draw the second loop you just grabbed under and up through the first loop.

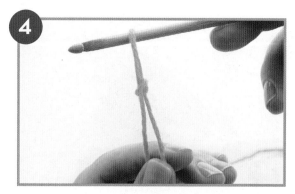

Slide your fingers out. Pull your hook up while gently pulling both ends of the yarn down.

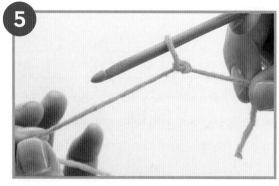

Pull the ends of the yarn to tighten the slip knot close to your hook.

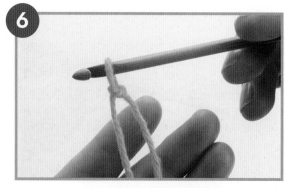

With a finished slip knot around your hook, you are ready to start crocheting.

Chain Stitch (ch)

Crochet often begins with a series of chain stitches used to make up the first row.
This is called the foundation chain and is the basic start to most crochet projects.

Start with a slip knot on your hook. Hold the yarn tail for tension.

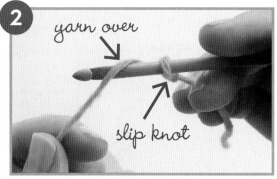

Bring the working yarn (the yarn coming from the ball) over your hook from back to front. This is called yarn over (yo).

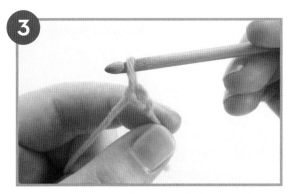

Draw this section of yarn back through the slip knot. You will have 1 new loop on your hook when your first chain stitch is complete.

Yarn over again.

Draw this section of yarn through the loop on your hook. You will have 1 new loop on your hook each time you complete a chain stitch.

Repeat steps 2–3 until your foundation chain has the required number of chain stitches.

Tension

Tension keeps your stitches neat and consistent. Make sure the chains in your foundation chain are even and loose enough to allow your hook back into those chains for the next row.

Too loose   **Too tight**   **Just right**

Slip Stitch (sl st)

The slip stitch is one of the most basic crochet stitches and is often used for joining.

Start with a foundation chain on your hook. Insert your hook from front to back into the second chain from your hook. There are 2 loops on your hook.

Yarn over, bringing the working yarn over your hook from back to front.

Draw the yarn through both loops on your hook. You will have 1 new loop on your hook when your first slip stitch is complete.

Counting Chains

Crochet patterns usually begin by telling you the number of chains needed for the foundation chain.

Front

Back

Identifying the Front and Back

The front of the foundation chain looks like a braid with a series of Vs. The back side of the foundation chain has a vertical ridge of bumps running down the middle from your hook to the end of the chain. Count chains from the front side.

Counting

Begin counting from the top of the foundation chain. (You can also count from the bottom up.) Do not count the loop on your hook or the slip knot on the bottom. Count only completed, V-shaped chain stitches. This example has 13 completed chain stitches.

Tip: When creating a long foundation chain, it is helpful to use stitch markers every 10 or 20 stitches to make counting easier.

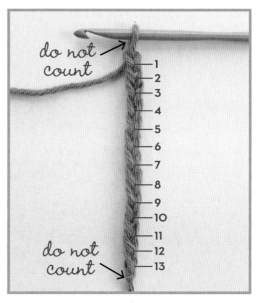

do not count

do not count

1
2
3
4
5
6
7
8
9
10
11
12
13

Turning Chains (tch)

Stitch	Number of Turning Chains
Slip stitch	0
Single crochet	1
Half double crochet	2
Double crochet	3
Treble crochet	4

Each crochet stitch requires a specific number of turning chains at the beginning or end of a row. The number of extra stitches needed for the turning chain is added to the number needed for the foundation chain.

Single Crochet (sc)

How to single crochet:

To begin a row of single crochet, first stitch a foundation chain to the desired length. Add 1 extra chain stitch for the turning chain.

Insert your hook from front to back into the second chain stitch from your hook. There will now be 2 loops on your hook.

Yarn over. Draw this yarn through the first loop on your hook. There will be 2 loops on your hook.

3

Yarn over again and draw this yarn through both loops on your hook. You will have 1 loop remaining on your hook when your first single crochet is complete.

4

insert your hook into this stitch

Insert your hook into the next chain stitch. Repeat steps 2–3 to complete another single crochet stitch.

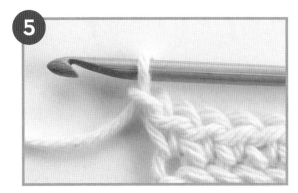

5

Repeat step 4, working a single crochet stitch into each chain. At the end of the row, make 1 chain stitch for the turning chain.

6

insert your hook into this stitch

Turn your work so that the opposite side faces you. Insert your hook into the first single crochet stitch of the previous row and repeat steps 2–3. (Skip the turning chain.)

7

Insert your hook into the next stitch and repeat steps 2–3, working a single crochet stitch into each single crochet of the previous row.

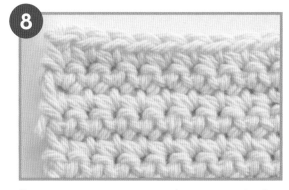

8

Repeat step 7 to continue the pattern. At the end of all rows, chain 1 for the turning chain, turn, and insert your hook into the next stitch.

Half Double Crochet (hdc)

How to half double crochet:

To begin a row of half double crochet, first stitch a foundation chain to the desired length. Add 2 extra chain stitches for the turning chain.

insert your hook into this stitch

Yarn over. With this yarn over, insert your hook into the third chain stitch from your hook. There will be 3 loops on your hook.

Yarn over again. Draw the yarn through the first loop only. There will still be 3 loops on your hook.

3

Yarn over and draw the yarn through all 3 loops on your hook.

4

You will have 1 loop on your hook when your first half double crochet stitch is complete.

5

insert your hook into this stitch

Yarn over. With this yarn over, insert your hook into the next chain stitch. There will be 3 loops on your hook. Repeat steps 2–4 to complete another half double crochet stitch.

6

Repeat step 5, working a half double crochet stitch into each chain stitch. At the end of the row, chain 2 for the turning chain.

7

insert your hook into this stitch

Turn your work so that the opposite side faces you. Yarn over and insert your hook into the second stitch. (The turning chain counts as the first half double crochet stitch in this row.) Repeat steps 2–4 to complete the stitch.

8

Repeat step 5 to continue making half double crochet stitches into each stitch of the previous row. At the end of this and all subsequent rows, chain 2 for the turning chain and turn.

Double Crochet (dc)

How to double crochet:

To begin a row of double crochet, first stitch a foundation chain to the desired length. Add 3 extra chain stitches for the turning chain.

insert your hook into this stitch

Yarn over. With this yarn over, insert your hook into the fourth chain stitch from your hook. There will be 3 loops on your hook.

Yarn over. Draw the yarn through the first loop on your hook. There will be 3 loops on your hook.

3

Yarn over. Draw the yarn through the first 2 loops on your hook only. There will now be 2 loops on your hook.

4

Yarn over again. Draw the yarn through the remaining 2 loops on your hook. You will have 1 loop on your hook when your first double crochet stitch is complete.

5

insert your hook into this stitch

Yarn over. Insert your hook into the next chain stitch. Repeat steps 2–4 to complete another double crochet stitch.

6

Repeat step 5, working a double crochet stitch into each chain stitch. At the end of the row, chain 3 for the turning chain. Turn your work so that the opposite side faces you.

7

insert your hook into this stitch

Yarn over and insert your hook into the second stitch. (The turning chain counts as the first double crochet stitch in this row.) Repeat steps 2–4 to complete the stitch.

8

Repeat step 5 to continue making double crochet stitches into each stitch of the previous row. At the end of this and all subsequent rows, chain 3 for the turning chain and turn.

Treble Crochet (tr)

How to treble crochet:

To begin a row of treble crochet, first stitch a foundation chain to the desired length. Add 4 extra chain stitches for the turning chain.

Yarn over twice. Insert your hook into the fifth chain stitch from your hook. There will be 4 loops on your hook.

Yarn over once. Draw the yarn through the first loop on your hook. There will be 4 loops on your hook.

3

Yarn over once. Draw the yarn through the first 2 loops on your hook. There will be 3 loops on your hook.

4

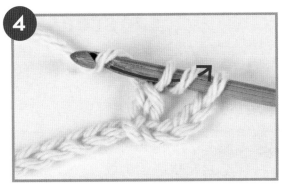

Yarn over once. Draw the yarn through the first 2 loops on your hook again. There will be 2 loops on your hook.

5

Yarn over. Draw the yarn through the remaining 2 loops on your hook. You will have 1 loop on your hook when your first treble crochet stitch is complete.

6

insert your hook into this stitch

Yarn over twice and insert your hook into the next chain stitch. Repeat steps 2–5 to complete another treble crochet stitch.

7

insert your hook into this stitch

Repeat step 6, working a treble crochet stitch into each chain. At the end of the row, chain 4 for the turning chain. Turn your work so that the opposite side faces you. Yarn over twice and insert your hook into the second stitch. Repeat steps 2–5 to complete the treble crochet stitch.

8

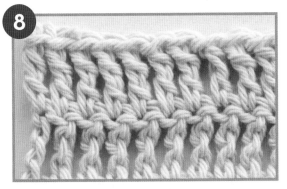

Repeat step 6 to continue making treble crochet stitches into each stitch of the previous row. At the end of this and all subsequent rows, chain 4 for the turning chain, yarn over twice, and insert your hook into the second stitch.

Decreasing Stitches (dec)

To decrease within a row, combine multiple stitches together.

Single Crochet Decrease

insert your hook into this stitch

Insert your hook into the next stitch as you would to start a single crochet.

Yarn over and draw the yarn through the stitch. There are now 2 loops on your hook.

Insert your hook into the next stitch. Yarn over and draw the yarn through the stitch. There are 3 loops on your hook.

Yarn over and draw the yarn through all 3 loops on your hook. You will have 1 loop on your hook when your first decrease is complete.

Double Crochet Decrease

Yarn over and insert your hook into the next stitch. Yarn over and draw the yarn through the stitch. Yarn over and draw the yarn through the first 2 loops. You will have 2 loops on your hook.

Yarn over and insert your hook into the next stitch. Yarn over and draw the yarn through the stitch. Yarn over and draw the yarn through the first 2 loops. You will have 3 loops on your hook.

3

Yarn over and draw the yarn through all 3 loops on your hook. You will have 1 loop on your hook when your first decrease is complete.

Increasing Stitches (inc)

To increase within a row, work multiple stitches into the same stitch.

Single Crochet Increase

1

Insert your hook back into the same stitch you did your last single crochet in. Work another single crochet into that same stitch.

2

You will have 1 loop on your hook when your first single crochet increase is complete.

Double Crochet Increase

1

Insert your hook back into the same stitch in the previous row. Work another double crochet into that same stitch.

2

You will have 1 loop on your hook when your first double crochet increase is complete.

Front & Back Loops (FL & BL)

Working into the front or back loop only will create a unique texture and line.
These examples use half double crochet, but you can use these techniques with other stitches.

Tip: When your crochet work is in front of you, the front loop is the loop closer to you, while the back loop is farther from you.

front loop   back loop

Front Loops

To work a half double crochet stitch into the front loop, yarn over and insert your hook into only the front loop facing you. Complete the stitch as usual.

Continue working half double crochet stitches into only the front loops of the stitches in the previous row until you reach the end of the row. This creates a line.

Back Loops

To work a half double crochet stitch into the back loop, yarn over and insert your hook into only the back loop facing away from you. Complete the stitch as usual.

Continue working half double crochet stitches into only the back loops of the stitches in the previous row until you reach the end of the row. This creates another line.

Working into Spaces

Some patterns will ask you to work into a space rather than a stitch of a previous row or round. This technique is demonstrated below using double crochet.

1 Start at the position where you want to work into a space. Yarn over.

2 Insert your hook from front to back into the space (instead of the stitch). Yarn over and pull the yarn through the space.

3 Finish your double crochet as usual. You will have 1 loop on your hook when your first double crochet stitch into the space is complete.

Here is the row finished with double crochet stitches worked into the spaces.

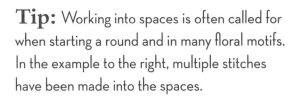

Tip: Working into spaces is often called for when starting a round and in many floral motifs. In the example to the right, multiple stitches have been made into the spaces.

Working in Rounds

To begin working in rounds, you have to first start with a center ring.
There are 2 different methods for starting a round, with a chain stitch ring or a magic circle.

Chain Stitch Ring

The chain stitch ring is made up of chain stitches that are joined together to form a ring. This method leaves a small opening in the center of your round.

Tip: Patterns will tell you how many chains to start with and what stitches to use. This example uses single crochet.

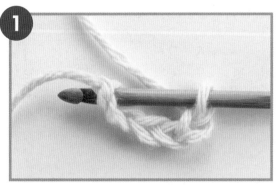

Chain 5 for a foundation chain. Insert your hook back into the first chain you made.

Work a slip stitch into that chain to form a ring.

Insert your hook into the center of the ring. Work a single crochet stitch into the ring.

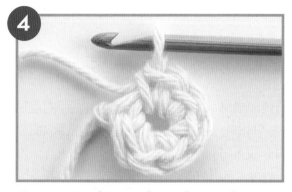

Continue working single crochet stitches into the ring until you have made the required number of stitches. (For this example, 6 single crochet stitches.)

5

Work a slip stitch into the first single crochet you made to close up the ring.

6

You are now ready to start a round. (See page 29.)

Magic Circle

The magic circle forms a ring with your yarn that your first round of stitches are attached to. The ends are pulled to leave no opening in the center. That's the magic!

Tip: A chain stitch ring can replace a magic circle in a pattern.

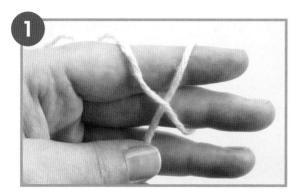

1

Loop the yarn around your fingers as shown to form an X.

2

Take your hook under the bottom strand of the X. Use your hook to draw the other strand under the bottom strand. It will form a loose loop on your hook.

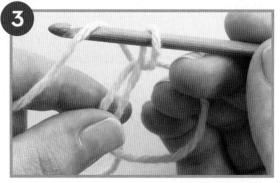

Remove the circle of yarn from your fingers. Yarn over. Draw the yarn through the loop on your hook. (This does not count as your first single crochet stitch.)

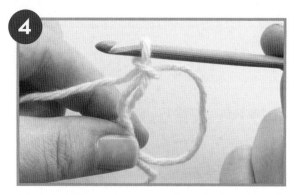

You should now have a circle with the tail and the working yarn on the left side.

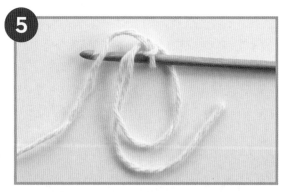

Insert your hook into the center of the circle. You are going to work a single crochet into that space. Yarn over and draw the yarn through the circle and tail. You will have 2 loops on your hook.

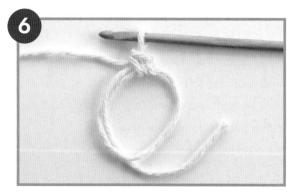

Yarn over again and draw the yarn through the remaining 2 loops on your hook. You will have 1 loop on your hook when your first single crochet stitch into the circle is complete.

Continue working the required number of single crochet stitches into the circle, making sure you are always working around the circle and the tail. If you run out of tail, pull it slightly. This closes the circle a little, but allows you to have a longer tail to work around.

When you have worked 6 single crochet stitches into the circle, pull the tail tightly to close the circle.

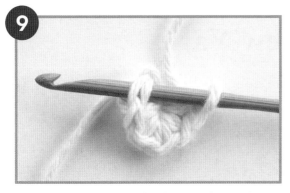

9 Insert your hook into the first single crochet stitch you made and make a slip stitch to close the circle.

10 With your slip stitch complete, you are now ready to start a round.

Starting a Round

To start a round, first begin by using either the chain stitch ring or magic circle method. This example used the magic circle method.

Round 1:

1 *insert your hook under these 2 loops*

Chain 1. Insert your hook under the top 2 loops of the first stitch and work a single crochet into that stitch.

2 Work 2 single crochets into each of the remaining stitches. (You will have 12 stitches.) Insert your hook back into the first stitch and make a slip stitch to close the round.

Rounds 2–6:

Each round increases by 6 stitches. The increases are evenly spaced in order to keep the circular shape. Close each round with a slip stitch back into the first stitch and then chain 1.

Round 2: Single crochet an increase in every other stitch for a total of 18 stitches.
Round 3: Single crochet an increase in every third stitch for a total of 24 stitches.
Round 4: Single crochet an increase in every fourth stitch for a total of 30 stitches.
Round 5: Single crochet an increase in every fifth stitch for a total of 36 stitches.
Round 6: Single crochet an increase in every sixth stitch for a total of 42 stitches.

For additional rounds, continue to evenly increase your rounds by 6 until your desired circumference.

Joining in New Yarn

At the End of a Row

To join in new yarn at the end of a row, work the last stitch with the old yarn until the final yarn over of the stitch. Yarn over with the new yarn.

Draw the new yarn through both loops on your hook. There is 1 loop on your hook. Continue stitching with the new yarn as usual.

In the Middle of a Row

To join in new yarn in the middle of a row, work the last stitch with the old yarn until the final yarn over of the stitch. Yarn over with the new yarn.

Draw the new yarn through both loops on your hook. There is 1 loop on your hook. Continue stitching with the new yarn as usual until you reach the end of the row.

Tip: Rather than leaving the tail of the old yarn in the middle of the row, you can work over the old yarn until you reach the end of the row. You can then weave in all yarn tails at the edges later.

Fastening Off

After completing your last stitch, cut the excess yarn, leaving several inches to weave the tail in later. Yarn over and draw the yarn tail through the loop on your hook.

Pull the yarn tail to tighten.

Weaving in the Tail

Thread one of your yarn tails into a blunt-tipped needle. Insert the needle into the first stitch and draw the yarn through.

Continue weaving the needle under and over the stitches around the edge.

Cut the yarn close to the final stitch when you're done weaving in the tail.

Abbreviations & Symbols

Crochet patterns often use abbreviations and symbols as shorthand to represent frequently used stitches and techniques. Use the guide below as you start to follow patterns using shorthand.

Abbreviations

alt	alternate
approx	approximately
beg	begin/beginning
bet	between
BL	back loop(s)
bo	bobble
BP	back post
BPdc	back post double crochet
BPsc	back post single crochet
BPtr	back post treble crochet
CC	contrasting color
ch	chain(s)
ch-sp	chain space
CL	cluster
cm	centimeter(s)
cont	continue
dc	double crochet
dec	decrease(s)/decreasing
dtr	double treble
edc	extended double crochet
ehdc	extended half double crochet
esc	extended single crochet
FL	front loop(s)
FP	front post
FPdc	front post double crochet
FPtr	front post treble crochet
hdc	half double crochet
hk	hook
inc	increase(s)/increasing
lp(s)	loop(s)
MC	main color
mm	millimeter(s)

p	picot
pc	popcorn
pat(s)	pattern(s)
pm	place marker
prev	previous
rem	remain/remaining
rep	repeat(s)
rnd(s)	round(s)
RS	right side
sc	single crochet
sl st	slip stitch
sk	skip
sp(s)	space(s)
st(s)	stitch(es)
tch	turning chain
tog	together
tr	treble crochet
WS	wrong side
yd(s)	yard(s)
yo	yarn over
"	inch(es)
[ ]	work instructions within brackets as many times as directed
( )	work instructions within parentheses as many times as directed
*	repeat the instructions following the single asterisk as directed
**	repeat the instructions between asterisks as many times as directed or repeat from a given set of instructions

Symbols

⬭	chain
•	slip stitch
X or †	single crochet
T	half double crochet
ꓕ	double crochet
ꓕ	treble crochet
⅄	sc2tog
⅄	sc3tog
⅄	dc2tog
⅄	dc3tog
⬡	3-dc cluster
⬡	3-hdc cluster/ puff st/bobble
⬡	5-dc popcorn
ⱱ	5-dc shell
⌒	ch-3 picot
J	front post dc
ꓴ	back post dc
⌢	worked in back loop only**
⌣	worked in front loop only**

**Symbol appears at base of stitch being worked.

CROCHET BABY PATTERNS

Bib with Pocket

Skill Level

EASY

Materials

Hook: 5.5 mm/U.S. H-8
Other: Button, pins (optional),
stitch markers, yarn needle

Stitches Used

Chain stitch (ch)
Crab stitch
Double crochet (dc)
Single crochet (sc)
Slip stitch (sl st)

Instructions

Bib

Ch 31.

Row 1: Sc in 2nd st from hook, sc in each st to end of row. Ch 1, turn.

Row 2: Sc in each st across. Ch 1, turn.

Rows 3–48: Repeat row 2.

Row 49: Sc in each of the next 7 sts, place stitch marker for strap to be worked later, sc in each of the remaining sts. Ch 1, turn.

Row 50: Sc in each of the next 7 sts. Ch 1, turn.

Rows 51–64: Sc in each st across. Turn.

Row 65: Ch 24, sc in 2nd ch from hook and in each of the next ch sts. Sc in each sc st from row 64. Ch 1, turn.

Rows 66–67: Sc in each st across. Ch 1, turn.

Row 68: Sc in each st across, leaving the 7 last sts unworked. Ch 1, turn.

Row 69: Sc in each st across. Ch 1, turn.

Row 70: Sc in each st across, ch 6, sk next 6 sts of unworked sts of row 67, dc in 7th sc of row 67 (buttonhole completed). Ch 1, turn.

Row 71: Sc in dc, sc in each stitch across row. Ch 1, turn.

Rows 72–73: Sc in each st across. At the end of row 73, fasten off and weave in ends.

Button Strap

Row 1: With the wrong side facing, join yarn to the stitch where stitch marker was placed in row 49. Ch 1, sc in same st, sc in each of the next 6 sts. Ch 1, turn.

Rows 2–23: Sc in each st across. At the end of row 23, fasten off and weave in ends.

Edges

With the right side facing, fold the bottom of the bib up so row 1 of the bib section rests on row 30 of the bib. Use pins if needed to keep the folded section in place.

Join yarn at the edge of bib. Ch 1, crab stitch in same st, and crab stitch evenly in each st along the edges of the bib. Work through both thicknesses along the folded areas of the bib and around straps at the top of bib. Work 3 sc in each corner. Join with a sl st to beginning crab stitch, fasten off and weave in ends.

Finishing

Sew button on with yarn between row 69 and row 70.

Tip: **Crab stitch:** Crab stitch is also called reverse single crochet because it is basically a single crochet worked the opposite way across the row. Instead of working right to left, crab stitch is worked left to right. To make the crab stitch: insert hook, yarn over and draw through first loop on hook, yarn over and draw through both loops on hook.

Looped Toy

Skill Level

EASY

Materials

Hook: 3.5 mm/U.S. E-4
Other: Polyester stuffing, yarn needle

Stitches Used

Chain stitch (ch)

Magic circle

Single crochet (sc)

Slip stitch (sl st)

Instructions

Small Outer Loop (make 2)

Make a magic circle, 6 sc into circle.

Round 1: Sc in each st around.

Continue repeating round 1, stuffing as you work, until tube measures 6 inches. Fasten off, leaving a long tail for sewing.

Closing the Loop

Bring both ends of tube together to form a loop and sew together using a yarn needle and the long tail of yarn. Fasten off and weave in ends.

Large Inner Loop

Make a magic circle, 8 sc into circle.

Round 1: Sc in each st around.

Continue repeating round 1, stuffing as you work, until tube measures 11 inches. Change colors for variation as desired at any point while working. Fasten off, leaving a long tail for sewing loop closed once desired length is reached.

Assembly

Slide the 2 smaller loops onto the large, unclosed loop (the tube). Bring both ends of the large loop together and sew together using a yarn needle and the long tail of yarn. Fasten off and weave in ends.

Cozy Cocoon

Skill Level

EASY

Materials

 1 skein

Hook: 5.5 mm/U.S. I-9
Other: Yarn needle

Stitches Used

Chain stitch (ch)

Double crochet (dc)

Magic circle

Single crochet (sc)

Slip stitch (sl st)

Instructions

Make a magic circle.

Round 1: Ch 3, 12 dc into circle. Sl st in top of ch 3 to join.

Round 2: Ch 2, 2 dc in each st around. Join with a sl st in first dc.

Round 3: Ch 2, *dc in 1 st, 2 dc in next st; repeat from * around. Join with a sl st in first dc.

Round 4: Ch 2, *dc in 2 sts, 2 dc in next st; repeat from * around. Join with a sl st in first dc.

Round 5: Ch 2, *dc in 3 sts, 2 dc in next st; repeat from * around. Join with a sl st in first dc.

Round 6: Ch 2, *dc in 4 sts, 2 dc in next st; repeat from * around. Join with a sl st in first dc.

Round 7: Ch 2, *dc in 5 sts, 2 dc in next st; repeat from * around. Join with a sl st in first dc.

Round 8: Ch 2, *dc in 13 sts, 2 dc in next st; repeat from * around. Join with a sl st in first dc.

Round 9: Ch 1, sc in join. *Skip 2 sts, 5 dc in next st, skip 2 sts, sc in next st; repeat from * around, ending skip 2, 5 dc in next st. Join with a sl st in first sc.

Round 10: Ch 3, 4 dc in same st. *Skip 2 dc, sc in next dc, 5 dc in next sc; repeat from * around, ending skip 2 dc, sc in next dc. Join with a sl st in top of ch 3.

Round 11: Sl st in 2 dc (don't pull these slip stitches tight), ch 1, sc in same dc, *5 dc in next sc, skip 2 dc, sc in next dc; repeat from * around, ending with 5 dc in next sc. Join with a sl st in first sc.

Rounds 12–43: Repeat rounds 10 and 11, ending with a round 11 when cocoon is desired size (typically around 21–22 inches).

Round 44: Ch 3, 5 dc in same st. *Skip 2 dc, sl st in next dc, 6 dc in next sc; repeat from * around, ending skip 2 dc, sl st in next dc. Join with a sl st in top of ch 3. Fasten off and weave in ends.

Hooded Scarf

Hook: 6.5 mm/U.S. K-10.5
Other: Buttons, yarn needle

Skill Level

INTERMEDIATE

Materials

 1 skein

Stitches Used

Chain stitch (ch)

Cluster (CL)

Double crochet (dc)

Single crochet (sc)

Slip stitch (sl st)

Whipstitch

Instructions

Hood

Ch 22.

Row 1: 2 dc in 4th ch from hook. *Skip 2 sts, (sc, 2 dc) in next ch. Repeat from * to end. Sc in last ch. Ch 2, turn.

Row 2: 2 dc in first st. *Skip 2 sts, (sc, 2 dc) in next st. Repeat from * to end. Sc in last st. Ch 2, turn.

Rows 3–35: Repeat row 2. Fasten off and weave in ends.

Fold in half and sew up the seam with a whipstitch.

Scarf

Ch 70.

Row 1: 2 dc in 4th ch from hook. *Skip 2 sts, (sc, 2 dc) in next ch. Repeat from * to end. Sc in last ch. Ch 2, turn.

Row 2: 2 dc in first st. *Skip 2 sts, (sc, 2 dc) in next st. Repeat from * to end. Sc in last st. Ch 2, turn.

Rows 3–9: Repeat row 2. Fasten off and weave in ends.

Attaching Scarf to Hood

Count 5 clusters in on the scarf and line up the third cluster with the first cluster on the edge of the hood. Whipstitch the scarf to the hood on the inside.

Edging

Attach yarn anywhere on the edge of the hood. Sc around edge, with 2 sc in corners. Complete 2 rows. Fasten off and weave in ends.

Sew on buttons to finish hooded scarf.

Tip: How to make the cluster: Work (sc, 2 dc) into the same chain or stitch.

Chevron Headband

Skill Level

INTERMEDIATE

Materials

LIGHT 3 2 skeins (1 of each color)

Hook: 3.5 mm/U.S. E-4
Other: Fold-over elastic, needle, thread

Stitches Used

Chain stitch (ch)
Double crochet (dc)
Single crochet (sc)
Single crochet 2 together (sc2tog)
Slip stitch (sl st)

Instructions

When changing color, do not cut yarn. Instead, bring up your color after each row. When you are ready to change color, you can use it into the last st with the previous color and then continue using the new color into the next row.

Ch 8.

Row 1: Sc in 2nd ch from hook. Sc in next 2 sts, 3 sc in next st, sc in next 3 sts. Ch 1, turn.

Rows 2–4: Sc2tog over next 2 sts, sc in next 2 sts, 3 sc in next st, sc in next 2 sts, sc2tog over next 2 sts. Ch 1, turn.

Join 2nd color.

Rows 5–8: Repeat rows 2–4.

Work with first color.

Rows 9–12: Repeat rows 2–4.

Continue working pattern until band is about 13" in length. Fasten off and weave in ends.

Adding Elastic

Cut elastic to about 4". Using thread and needle, sew elastic securely into place on each end of headband.

Bow (optional)

Ch 27.

Row 1: Dc in 4th ch from hook and in each st across. Ch 3, turn.

Row 2: Dc in 2nd st from hook and in each st across row. Ch 3, turn.

Row 3: Repeat row 2.

Finishing

Fold piece in half and join the two ends together with a slip stitch. Fasten off and weave in ends. Pinch together the middle to create a bow shape and wrap yarn tightly around the center until you are happy with the look. Knot yarn and weave in loose ends.

Sew this bow securely onto headband to finish.

Tip: **How to single crochet 2 together (sc2tog):** [Insert hook in next stitch, yarn over, draw yarn through stitch] 2 times, yarn over, draw yarn though all 3 loops on hook.

Bunny Blanket

Skill Level

INTERMEDIATE

Materials

 2 skeins (1 of each color)

Hook: 4 mm/U.S. G-6
Other: Black yarn scraps, polyester stuffing, stitch markers, yarn needle

Stitches Used

Chain stitch (ch)
Double crochet (dc)
Half double crochet (hdc)
Half double crochet 2 together (hdc2tog)
Half double crochet 3 together (hdc3tog)
Magic circle
Single crochet (sc)
Single crochet 2 together (sc2tog)
Slip stitch (sl st)

Tip: **Single crochet 2 together (sc2tog):** [Insert hook in next stitch, yarn over, draw yarn through stitch] twice, yarn over, draw yarn though all 3 loops on hook.

Instructions

Ears

Make 2 with color 1 for outer ears, and 2 with color 2 for inner ears.

Ch 15.

Row 1: Dc in 4th ch from hook and in each of next 10 sts. 6 dc in last ch and continue working across opposite side of ch. Dc in each of the next 11 sts, ch 2 and sl st in last ch. Fasten off, leaving a long end for sewing.

Ear Assembly

Place 1 inner ear and 1 outer ear together with right sides facing out, matching stitches. With color 1, join with a sl st in bottom right corner through both pieces. Ch 1 and working through both, sc in each st around until reaching bottom left corner. Fasten off, leaving a long end for sewing.

Head

With color 1, make a magic circle. Work 6 sc into magic circle.

Use stitch marker to mark first st in each round, moving it up while you work.

Round 1: 2 sc in each st around.

Round 2: *2 sc in next st, sc in next st. Repeat from * around.

Round 3: *2 sc in next st, sc in next 2 sts. Repeat from * around.

Round 4: *2 sc in next st, sc in next 3 sts. Repeat from * around.

Round 5: *2 sc in next st, sc in next 3 sts. Repeat from * around.

Rounds 6–11: Sc in each st around. Do not fasten off. Drop loop that will be picked up later.

Attach ears: Use stitch markers to mark placement of ears on round 3. For each ear, pull the long ends of yarn left for sewing through the head and knot inside to secure. Sew eyes and nose on head using yarn scraps and a yarn needle. Fasten off and weave in ends.

Round 12: Pick up dropped loop at end of round 11, *sc2tog over next 2 sts, sc in next 6 sts. Repeat from * around.

Round 13: *Sc2tog over next 2 sts, sc in next 3 sts. Repeat from * around.

Round 14: *Sc2tog over next 2 sts, sc in next 2 sts. Repeat from * around.

Fill head with stuffing.

With the head facing forward, flatten the last round of the head. The blanket row will be started next, and your hook should be positioned directly under the right ear. If it is not, sc to that point before beginning the blanket rows.

Tip: **Half double crochet 2 together (hdc2tog):** [Yarn over, insert hook in next st, yarn over and draw up a loop] twice as indicated, yarn over, draw yarn through all loops on hook.

Blanket

Row 1: Ch 2, work through double thickness of the last round of the head, hdc in each st across. Ch 2, turn.

Rows 2–16: 2 hdc in first st, hdc in next sts until last st. 2 hdc in last st. Ch 2, turn.

Row 17: Hdc in each st across. Ch 2, turn.

Rows 18–35: Hdc2tog over first 2 sts, hdc in next sts until last 2 sts, hdc2tog over last 2 sts. Ch 2, turn.

Row 36: Hdc3tog over next 3 sts, fasten off and weave in ends.

Edging

Join yarn to first st of blanket row 1 and sc evenly across the edge of the blanket, working 2 sc in each corner. Fasten off and weave in ends.

Tip: **Half double crochet 3 together (hdc3tog):** [Yarn over, insert hook in next st, yarn over and draw up a loop] 3 times as indicated, yarn over, draw yarn through all loops on hook.

Teething Biscuits

Skill Level

BEGINNER

Materials

MEDIUM 4

Hook: 4.5 mm/U.S. 7

Other: Yarn needle

Stitches Used

Chain stitch (ch)

Half double crochet (hdc)

Single crochet (sc)

Slip stitch (sl st)

Instructions

Biscuits (make 2)

Ch 10.

Round 1: 2 hdc in 2nd ch from hook. Hdc in each ch until last st, 4 hdc in last st. Continue working 1 hdc around in back loops of original ch until last st. 2 hdc in last st. Join with a sl st to close round.

Round 2: Ch 2, 2 hdc in each of the next 2 sts, hdc in next 7 sts, 2 hdc in each of the next 4 sts, hdc in next 7 sts, 2 hdc in each of the next 2 sts. Join with a sl st and fasten off.

Finishing

Hold 2 biscuits together with right sides facing out. Attach yarn through both and sc in each st around, working sts through both biscuits to join. Fasten off and weave in ends.

Tip: Biscuits work best for babies when they are frozen. Keep them in the freezer until needed and then let baby chew on them to soothe gums.

Sun Hat

Skill Level

INTERMEDIATE

Materials

Hook: 5.5 mm/U.S. I-9
Other: Yarn needle

Stitches Used

Chain stitch (ch)

Double crochet (dc)

Half double crochet (hdc)

Magic circle

Puff stitch

Single crochet (sc)

Slip stitch (sl st)

Tip: How to make the puff stitch
[Yarn over, draw up a loop] 3 times, yarn over and draw through all 7 loops on hook.

Instructions

Make a magic circle.

Round 1: Ch 1, 10 hdc into magic circle. Sl st to first hdc to join.

Round 2: Ch 1, 2 hdc in each st around. Sl st to first hdc to join.

Round 3: Ch 1, *2 hdc in next st, hdc in next st. Rep from * around. Sl st to first hdc to join.

Round 4: Ch 1, *2 hdc in next st, hdc in each of the next 2 sts. Rep from * around. Sl st to first hdc to join.

Round 5: Ch 1, *2 hdc in next st, hdc in each of the next 3 sts. Rep from * around. Sl st to first hdc to join.

Round 6: Ch 1, hdc in each st around. Sl st in first hdc to join.

Round 7: Ch 1, *sc, ch 1, skip the next st, sc, ch 2, skip the next 2 sts, dc, ch 1, skip the next st, dc, ch 2, skip the next 2 sts. Rep from * around. Sl st to first sc to join.

Round 8: Sl st in the first ch-1 sp, ch 2, *(puff, ch 1, puff, ch 1, puff, ch 2) in the ch-1 sp. Sc in the next ch-1 sp, ch 2. Rep from * around. Sl st in first puff to join.

Round 9: Sl st into the first ch-1 sp, ch 2, *dc in ch-1 sp, ch 1, dc in next ch-1 sp, ch 2, sc in next ch-2 sp, ch 1, sc in next ch-2 sp, ch 2. Rep from * around. Sl st in first dc to join.

Round 10: Sl st into the first ch-1 sp, ch 1, *sc, ch 2, (puff, ch 1, puff, ch 1, puff, ch 2) in ch-1 sp. Rep from * around. Sl st in first sc to join.

Round 11: Sl st into the first ch-1 sp, ch 1, *sc in ch-2 sp, ch 2, dc in next ch-1 sp, ch 1, dc in next ch-1 sp, ch 2, sc in next ch-2 sp, ch 1, skip next sc. Rep from * around. Sl st in first sc to join.

Round 12: Sl st into the next 2 ch sts, dc in next ch-1 sp. Ch 1, *sc, ch 2, (puff, ch 1, puff, ch 1, puff, ch 2) in next ch-1 sp. Rep from * around. Sl st in first sc to join.

Round 13: Repeat round 11.

Round 14: Repeat round 12.

Round 15: Ch 1, *2 hdc in next st, hdc in next st. Rep from * around in each st and ch st. Sl st in first hdc to join.

Rounds 16–19: Ch 1, hdc in each st around. Sl st in first hdc to join. Fasten off and weave in ends at the end of round 19.

Pacifier Clips

Skill Level

EASY

Materials

Hook: 3.5 mm/U.S. E-4

Other: Metal pacifier clips, yarn needle

Stitches Used

Chain stitch (ch)
Double crochet (dc)
Popcorn stitch
Single crochet (sc)

Instructions

Pattern 1 (here in orange):

Row 1: With a slip knot on your hook, insert hook through top of pacifier clip and sc 5 times onto the clip. Ch 1, turn.

Row 2: Sc in each st across. Ch 3, turn.

Row 3: 4 dc in 3rd st from hook. Dc in last st of row. Ch 3, turn.

Row 4: 4 dc in center of 4 dc from previous row. Dc in last st of row. Ch 3, turn.

Rows 5–15: Repeat row 4.

Row 16: 4 dc in center of 4 dc from previous row. Dc in last st of row. Ch 1, turn.

Row 17: Sc in each st across row. Ch 1, turn.

Row 18: Sc in first 3 sts, ch 16, sc back into same st to create a loop, sc in last 2 sts. Fasten off and weave in ends.

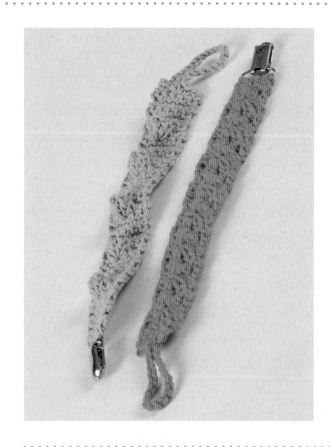

Tip: How to make the popcorn stitch
Work 5 dc stitches in the same st, drop the loop from your hook, insert hook from front to back under the top 2 loops of the first dc group, grab the dropped loop with your hook and pull through the stitch.

Pattern 2 (here in blue):

Row 1: With a slip knot on your hook, insert hook through top of pacifier clip and sc 5 times onto the clip. Ch 1, turn.

Row 2: Sc in each st across. Ch 1, turn.

Rows 3–6: Repeat row 2.

Row 7: Sc in first 2 sts, popcorn st, sc in last 2 sts.

Rows 8–12: Repeat row 2.

Row 13: Repeat row 7.

Continue repeating until desired length and end with 5 rows of sc.

Final row: Sc in first 3 sts, ch 16, sc back into same st to create a loop, sc in last 2 sts. Fasten off and weave in ends.

Striped Baby Blanket

Skill Level

EASY

Materials

3 skeins (1 in each color)

Hook: 6 mm/U.S. J-10

Other: Yarn needle

Stitches Used

Chain stitch (ch)

Double crochet (dc)

Single crochet (sc)

Instructions

Using color 1, ch 74 (or a multiple of 3 + 2).

Row 1: Sc in the 2nd ch from hook and in each ch across. Ch 3, turn.

Row 2: Dc in first st, *skip next 2 sts, 3 dc into next st. Repeat from * across row until last st, 2 dc in last st. Ch 3, turn.

Row 3: 3 dc into first space of previous row. *3 dc in next space of previous row. Repeat from * across row, ending with 1 dc in last st. Change to color 2. Ch 3, turn.

Row 4: Dc in first st. *3 dc in space from previous row. Repeat from * across row, ending with 2 dc in final st. Ch 3, turn.

Row 5: 3 dc into first space of previous row. *3 dc in next space of previous row. Repeat from * across row, ending with 1 dc in last st. Change to color 3. Ch 3, turn.

Row 6: Dc in first st. *3 dc in space from previous row. Repeat from * across row, ending with 2 dc in final st. Ch 3, turn.

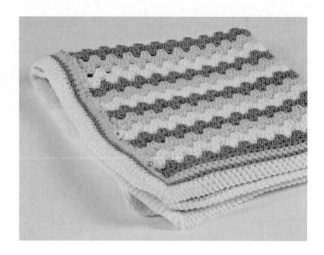

Row 7: 3 dc into first space of previous row. *3 dc in next space of previous row. Repeat from * across row, ending with 1 dc in last st. Change to color 1. Ch 3, turn.

Row 8: Dc in first st. *3 dc in space from previous row. Repeat from * across row, ending with 2 dc in final st. Ch 3, turn.

Row 9: Repeat rows 3–8 until the blanket is desired size. Fasten off and weave in all ends.

Border

Attach yarn to edge and sc evenly along edges of blanket, using 3 sc in each corner. Repeat as desired. Fasten off and weave in all ends.

Heart Mobile

Skill Level

INTERMEDIATE

Materials

Hook: 3.5 mm/U.S. E-4
Other: Center section of wood embroidery hoop, polyester stuffing, stitch markers, yarn needle

Stitches Used

Chain stitch (ch)
Magic circle
Single crochet (sc)
Single crochet 2 together (sc2tog)

Instructions

Small Heart (make 2 heart tops)

Make a magic circle.

Round 1: Work 5 sc into the magic circle.

Use a stitch marker to mark the first st of each round. Move marker up as you work.

Round 2: 2 sc in each st around.

Round 3: *2 sc in next st, sc in next st. Repeat from * around.

Round 4: Sc in each st around. Round 4 is the end of the first heart top. Fasten off, but leave end to sew the space between the heart tops together. Do not fasten off after completing the 2nd heart top; continue working into next round.

Round 5: Join the 2nd heart top to the first and sc in each st around both tops. Sew up the space in between with a yarn needle and the tail left from round 4.

Round 6: Sc in next 5 sts, sc2tog over next 2 sts, sc in next st, sc2tog over next 2 sts, sc in next 10 sts, sc2tog over next 2 sts, sc in next st, sc2tog over next 2 sts, sc in last 5 sts.

Round 7: *Sc in next 4 sts, sc2tog over next 2 sts, sc in next st, sc2tog over next 2 sts, sc in next 2 sts, sc2tog over next 2 sts. Repeat from * around.

Round 8: Sc in next 2 sts, sc2tog over next 2 sts, sc in next 2 sts, sc2tog over next 2 sts, sc in next 4 sts, sc2tog over next 2 sts, sc in next 2 sts, sc2tog over next 2 sts, sc in next 2 sts.

Round 9: Sc in next 2 sts, [sc2tog over next 2 sts] 2 times, sc in next 4 sts, [sc2tog over next 2 sts] 2 times, sc in next 2 sts.

Begin to stuff the heart with polyester stuffing.

Round 10: *Sc in next 4 sts, sc2tog over next 2 sts. Repeat from * around.

Round 11: *Sc in next 3 sts, sc2tog over next 2 sts. Repeat from * around. Finish stuffing the heart.

Round 12: *Sc in next 2 sts, sc2tog over next 2 sts. Repeat from * around.

Round 13: [Sc2tog] 2 times. Fasten off and use the length of yarn to completely close opening by sewing closed with yarn needle.

Repeat to make additional small hearts.

Large Heart (make 2 heart tops)

Make a magic circle.

Round 1: Work 5 sc into magic circle.

Use a stitch marker to mark the first st of each round. Move up marker as you work.

Round 2: 2 sc in each st around.

Round 3: *2 sc in next st, sc in next st. Repeat from * around.

Round 4: *2 sc in next st, sc in next 2 sts. Repeat from * around.

Round 5: *2 sc in next st, sc in next 3 sts. Repeat from * around.

Rounds 6–8: Sc in each st around. Round 8 is the end of the first heart top. Fasten off but leave end to sew the space between the heart tops together. Do not fasten off after the end of the 2nd heart top; continue working yarn into next round.

Round 9: Join the 2nd heart top and the first together and sc in each st around both.

Round 10: Sc in the next 10 sts, sc2tog over next 2 sts, sc in next st, sc2tog over next 2 sts, sc in next 20 sts, sc2tog over next 2 sts, sc in next st, sc2tog over next 2 sts, sc in last 10 sts.

Round 11: *Sc in next 9 sts, sc2tog over next 2 sts, sc in next st, sc2tog over next 2 sts, sc in next 7 sts, sc2tog over next 2 sts. Repeat from * around.

Round 12: Sc in next 7 sts, sc2tog over next 2 sts, sc in next 2 sts, sc2tog over next 2 sts, sc in next 14 sts, sc2tog over next 2 sts, sc in next 2 sts, sc2tog over next 2 sts, sc in last 7 sts.

Round 13: *Sc2tog over next 2 sts, sc in next 4 sts, sc2tog over next 2 sts, sc in next 2 sts, sc2tog over next 2 sts, sc in next 6 sts. Repeat from * around.

Round 14: Sc in next 5 sts, sc2tog over next 2 sts, sc in next st, sc2tog over next 2 sts, sc in next 10 sts, sc2tog over next 2 sts, sc in next st, sc2tog over next 2 sts, sc in next 5 sts.

Round 15: *Sc in next 4 sts, sc2tog over next 2 sts, sc in next st, sc2tog over next 2 sts, sc in next 2 sts, sc2tog over next 2 sts. Repeat from * around.

Round 16: Sc in next 2 sts, sc2tog over next 2 sts, sc in next 2 sts, sc2tog over next 2 sts, sc in next 4 sts, sc2tog over next 2 sts, sc in next 2 sts, sc2tog over next 2 sts, sc in next 2 sts.

Round 17: Sc in next 2 sts, [sc2tog over next 2 sts] 2 times, sc in next 4 sts, [sc2tog over next 2 sts] 2 times, sc in next 2 sts.

Begin to stuff heart with polyester stuffing.

Round 18: *Sc in next 4 sts, sc2tog over next 2 sts. Repeat from * around.

Round 19: *Sc in next 3 sts, sc2tog over next 2 sts. Repeat from * around.

Finish stuffing heart.

Round 20: *Sc in next 2 sts, sc2tog over next 2 sts. Repeat from * around. Fasten off and use the length of yarn to completely close opening by sewing closed with yarn needle.

Round 21: [Sc2tog] 2 times. Fasten off and use the length of yarn to completely close opening by sewing closed with yarn needle.

Assembly

Make 1 large heart and 9 small hearts in various colors. With different lengths of yarn, attach the small hearts to wooden embroidery hoop. Wrap yarn around hoop to decorate the hoop. Use equal lengths of yarn to create a hook at top of hoop for hanging, and hang the large heart down the center of the hoop.

Baby Rattle

Skill Level

EASY

Materials

Hook: 3.75 mm/U.S. F-5
Other: 2 large jingle bells, polyester stuffing, stitch marker, yarn needle

Stitches Used

Magic circle
Single crochet (sc)
Single crochet 2 together (sc2tog)

Instructions

Make a magic circle, 6 sc in magic circle.

From here on, place marker in beginning st of each round to keep track of rounds.

Round 1: 2 sc in each st.

Round 2: *2 sc in next st, sc in next st. Rep from * around to marker.

Round 3: *2 sc in next st, sc in each of the next 2 sts. Rep from * around to marker.

Round 4: *2 sc in next st, sc in each of the next 3 sts. Rep from * around to marker.

Rounds 5–8: Sc in each st around to marker.

Round 9: *Sc2tog in next 2 sts, sc in each of the next 3 sts. Rep from * around to marker.

Round 10: *Sc2tog in next 2 sts, sc in each of the next 2 sts. Rep from * around to marker. Stuff and add 1 bell now.

Round 11: *Sc2tog in next 2 sts, sc in next st. Rep from * around to marker.

Rounds 12–21: Sc in each st to maker, stuffing as you go. Fasten off, leaving a long tail at end of round 21.

Make second ball of rattle by repeating rounds 1–12. Leave a long end and fasten off when done. Sew rattle handle to complete. Weave in all ends.

Tip: **Single crochet 2 together (sc2tog)**
[Insert hook in next st, yo, draw yarn through st] twice, yo, draw yarn though all loops on hook.

Hat and Mittens Set

Skill Level

EASY

Materials

Hook: 4 mm/U.S. G-6
Other: Stitch marker, yarn needle

Stitches Used

Back post half double crochet (BPhdc)

Chain stitch (ch)

Front post half double crochet (FPhdc)

Half double crochet (hdc)

Magic circle

Single crochet (sc)

Slip stitch (sl st)

Instructions

Hat

Make a magic circle. Ch 1 and work 9 hdc sts into the circle. Place marker in first st of each round to keep track of rounds. Move marker as you work.

Round 1: 2 hdc in each st around.

Round 2: *2 hdc in next st, hdc in next st. Repeat from * around to marker.

Round 3: *2 hdc in next st, hdc in each of next 2 sts. Repeat from * around to marker.

Round 4: Hdc in each st around to marker.

Round 5: Repeat roung 4 until the hat measures 5" from where you began to the edge. Finish hat by sc in 2nd to last st of final round, and sl st in last st of final round. Do not fasten off.

Edging

Round 1: Ch 1, sc in same st as ch 1 and sc in each st around. Sl st in beginning sc to join.

Round 2: Repeat round 1.

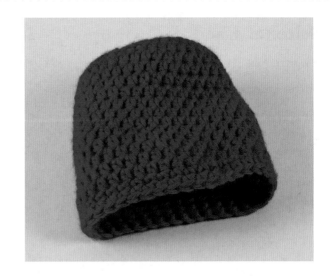

Fasten off and weave in ends.

Mittens (make 2)

Make a magic circle, ch 1 and work 8 hdc into the circle.

Place a marker in the first st of each round to keep track of rounds. Move marker as you work.

Round 1: 2 hdc in each st around.

Round 2: *Sc in next st, hdc in next st. Repeat from * around to marker.

Rounds 3–11: Hdc in each st around.

Tip: Back post half double crochet (BPhdc): Yo and insert hook from back to front under post of st in previous round. Yo and draw yarn around post. Yo and draw yarn through first 2 loops on hook. Yo and draw through remaining 2 loops on hook.

Round 12: Hdc in each st around until last 2 sts. Sc in 2nd to last st, sl st in last st.

(Mittens should measure about 3" in length. Add or subtract rounds to adjust size, if needed.)

Round 13: Ch 2, *FPhdc in next st, BPhdc in next st. Repeat from * around to marker, sl st in first FPhdc to join.

Rounds 14–15: Repeat round 13, working the

FPhdc in previous FPhdc and the BPhdc in previous BPhdc.

Fasten off and weave in ends.

Ties (make 2)

Ch 60. Fasten off and weave in the tails. Thread chain through the mittens between the front and back post stitches. Finish by tying in a bow.

Tip: Front post half double crochet (FPhdc): Yo and insert hook from front to back under post of st in previous round. Yo and draw yarn around post. Yo and draw yarn through first 2 loops on hook. Yo and draw yarn through remaining 2 loops on hook.

Baby Blocks

Skill Level

EASY

Materials

Hook: 3.5 mm/U.S. E-4
Other: Polyester stuffing, yarn needle

Stitches Used

Chain stitch (ch)

Double crochet (dc)

Magic circle

Slip stitch (sl st)

Treble crochet (tr)

Whipstitch

Instructions

Make 6 squares for each block.

Make a magic circle.

Round 1: Ch 3, 2 dc, 1 tr into circle. *3 dc, 1 tr into circle. Rep from * twice more and join with a sl st to the top of beg ch 3. Change color.

Round 2: Ch 3, *dc in each dc to tr, (2 dc, tr, 2 dc) in tr. Rep from * 3 more times, dc in each dc across to beg ch 3, join with a sl st to the top of beg ch 3. Change color.

Round 3: Rep round 2. Fasten off and weave in ends.

Assembly

Once 6 squares are completed, use yarn needle and lengths of yarn to whipstitch the squares together to shape block. Before closing off final edge, stuff block with polyester stuffing.

Cuffed Booties

Hook: 3.5 mm/U.S. E-4
Other: Yarn needle

Skill Level

INTERMEDIATE

Materials

Stitches Used

Back post half double crochet (BPhdc)

Chain stitch (ch)

Double crochet (dc)

Front post half double crochet (FPhdc)

Half double crochet (hdc)

Slip stitch (sl st)

Tip: **Back post half double crochet (BPhdc):** Yarn over, insert hook from back to front to back under post of stitch, yarn over and pull up loop, yarn over and draw through all 3 loops on hook.

Instructions

Booties (make 2)

Ch 10.

Round 1: 2 hdc in 3rd ch from hook. 1 hdc in remaining chains with 6 hdc worked in last ch. Continue working along the underside of the chain, working 1 hdc in each ch st until the last ch. Work 3 hdc in last ch, sl st to join in top of first hdc.

Round 2: Ch 2, hdc in same st. 2 hdc in each of the next 2 sts. Hdc in the next 7 sts, 2 hdc in each of the next 5 sts, hdc in each of the next 6 sts.

Finish round with 2 hdc in each of the next 2 sts, sl st to join in the top of ch 2 to join.

Round 3: Ch 2 (work in back loops only for this round) 1 hdc in same st and in each st around. Sl st to top of ch 2 to join.

Round 4: Ch 2, hdc in each st around. Sl st in top of ch 2 to join.

Round 5: Repeat round 4. Do not fasten off.

Toe of Bootie

These stitches will be worked in 16 sts in the front half of the bootie. To find the center, fold the bootie in half length-wise and count 8 sts both ways from the center mark. These are the 16 sts the toe of the bootie is worked in.

Join new yarn in first of the 16 sts just found.

Row 1: Ch 2 (counts as first st). Work 15 dc in each of the next 15 sts, each time leaving the last loop of the dc st on the hook while working the next st. Pull through all sts on hook at final st and finish with a yarn over and pull through. Fasten off.

Cuff

Pick up loop at the back of bootie from round 5.

Round 1: Ch 2, work hdc in each st around including sides of the 16 dc toe. Sl st to top of ch 2 to join.

Round 2: Ch 2, *FPhdc in next st, BPhdc in next st; repeat from * around. Sl st in top of ch 2 to join.

Rounds 3–5: Repeat round 2. Fasten off and weave in all ends.

Tip: **Front post half double crochet (FPhdc):** Yarn over, insert hook under post of stitch, yarn over and pull up a loop, yarn over and draw through all 3 loops on hook.